✳Proverbs

Volume 1

DISCOVER TOGETHER BIBLE STUDY SERIES

Psalms: Discovering Authentic Worship
Proverbs: Discovering Ancient Wisdom for a Postmodern World, Volume 1
Proverbs: Discovering Ancient Wisdom for a Postmodern World, Volume 2
Ecclesiastes: Discovering Meaning in a Meaningless World
Daniel: Discovering the Courage to Stand for Your Faith
Luke: Discovering Healing in Jesus' Words to Women
Galatians: Discovering Freedom in Christ Through Daily Practice
Ephesians: Discovering Your Identity and Purpose in Christ
Philippians: Discovering Joy Through Relationship
James: Discovering God's Delight in a Lived-Out Faith
1 Peter: Discovering Encouragement in Troubling Times
Revelation: Discovering Life for Today and Eternity

Leader's guides are available at www.discovertogetherseries.com

A Discover Together
BIBLE STUDY

Proverbs

Discovering Ancient Wisdom
for a Postmodern World
Volume 1

Sue Edwards

Kregel
Publications

Proverbs: Discovering Ancient Wisdom for a Postmodern World, Volume 1
© 2012 by Sue Edwards

Published by Kregel Publications, a division of Kregel Inc., 2450 Oak Industrial Dr. NE, Grand Rapids, MI 49505.

Previously published by Kregel Publications as *Proverbs: Ancient Wisdom for a Postmodern World, Volume 1,* © 2007 by Sue Edwards.

ISBN 978-0-8254-4307-7

Printed in the United States of America

18 19 20 21 22 23 24 25 / 6 5 4 3 2

Contents

How to Get the Most Out of a Discover Together Bible Study

Women today need Bible study to keep balanced, focused, and Christ-centered in their busy worlds. The tiered questions in *Proverbs: Discovering Ancient Wisdom for a Postmodern World, Volume 1* allow you to choose a depth of study that fits your lifestyle, which may even vary from week to week, depending on your schedule.

Just completing the basic questions will require about one and a half hours per lesson, and will provide a basic overview of the text. For busy women, this level offers in-depth Bible study with a minimum time commitment.

"Digging Deeper" questions are for those who want to, and make time to, probe the text even more deeply. Answering these questions may require outside resources such as an atlas, Bible dictionary, or concordance; you may be asked to look up parallel passages for additional insight; or you may be encouraged to investigate the passage using an interlinear Greek-English text or *Vine's Expository Dictionary*. This deeper study will challenge you to learn more about the history, culture, and geography related to the Bible, and to grapple with complex theological issues and differing views. Some with teaching gifts and an interest in advanced academics will enjoy exploring the depths of a passage, and might even find themselves creating outlines and charts and writing essays worthy of seminarians!

This inductive Bible study is designed for both individual and group discovery. You will benefit most if you tackle each week's lesson on your own, and then meet with other women to share insights, struggles, and aha moments. Bible study leaders will find free, downloadable leader's guides for each study, along with general tips for leading small groups, at www.discovertogetherseries.com.

Through short video clips, Sue Edwards shares personal insights to enrich your Bible study experience. You can watch these as you work through each lesson on your own, or your Bible study leader may want your whole study group to view them when you meet together. For ease of individual

viewing, a QR code, which you can simply scan with your smartphone, is provided in each lesson. Or you can go to www.discovertogetherseries.com and easily navigate until you find the corresponding video title. Woman-to-woman, these clips are meant to bless, encourage, and challenge you in your daily walk.

Choose a realistic level of Bible study that fits your schedule. You may want to finish the basic questions first, and then "dig deeper" as time permits. Take time to savor the questions, and don't rush through the application. Watch the videos. Read the sidebars for additional insight to enrich the experience. Note the optional passage to memorize and determine if this discipline would be helpful for you. Do not allow yourself to be intimidated by women who have more time or who are gifted differently.

Make your Bible study—whatever level you choose—top priority. Consider spacing your study throughout the week so that you can take time to ponder and meditate on what the Holy Spirit is teaching you. Do not make other appointments during the group Bible study. Ask God to enable you to attend faithfully. Come with an excitement to learn from others and a desire to share yourself and your journey. Give it your best, and God promises to join you on this adventure that can change your life.

Why Study Proverbs?

A proverb is a short, pithy couplet that teaches truth in a memorable way. Here are two examples:

> Anxiety weighs down the heart,
>   but a kind word cheers it up. (Proverbs 12:25)

> If anyone loudly blesses their neighbor early in the morning,
>   it will be taken as a curse. (Proverbs 27:14)

These short, pithy sayings begin in chapter 10 and end in chapter 29. The book of Proverbs is structured like a sandwich: these brief, memorable sayings are sandwiched between discourses at the beginning and at the end.

Here's another way to look at the organization:

Chapters 1–9	Incentives to seek wisdom from King Solomon
Chapters 10–29	Proverbs
Chapters 30–31	Insight on wisdom from Agur and King Lemuel's mother

 Introduction to Studying Proverbs (*8:38 minutes*).

WHAT YOU NEED TO KNOW ABOUT PROVERBS

Proverbs are *principles* that are true in general terms. They show us the way the world works and how to live wisely in it. If we live by wisdom

principles, we will not bring calamity on our heads by our own foolish actions and attitudes. Foolishness is the source of many people's problems. When we are our own worst enemies, we bring problems upon ourselves either by being unaware of how the world works or by ignoring what we know.

Proverbs are not *promises*. If we interpret proverbs as promises made to individuals, we're guilty of saying that God promises us something that he has not promised at all, and we confuse people regarding the Bible. It is crucial that we interpret the Bible in the way that the author intended.

A proverb is a wise saying—a few words pregnant with meaning. We must examine each word carefully and then dig for the overall meaning. When Benjamin Franklin coined the secular proverb, "A stitch in time saves nine," he was not promising that if you stitch up a hem before it unravels, it will never unravel again. He was explaining that if we attend to a situation early, we'll most likely encounter fewer problems later. Franklin was using figurative language to paint a picture of the way the world works. Solomon was his predecessor.

When mothers read the proverb, "Train up a child in the way he should go: and when he is old, he will not depart from it" (Proverbs 22:6 KJV), it's tempting to insist that God promises all prodigals will return. And God may give a mother that assurance. But God never makes that promise on the basis of this particular proverb. To insist that he has is to use bad interpretive principles. Instead, this proverb tells us that parents who do their best to understand their children and raise them in a godly home are *more likely* to see prodigals return to the faith than are those parents who never instructed their children in the first place. But turning to God is ultimately the child's choice. God does not override free choice for anyone. That's a principle he set in place from the foundation of the world.

Our task is to decipher the proverbs in order to learn timeless lessons about life, and then to live in light of their truth.

Proverbs' purpose is to propel us into a relationship with God so we might live out the truths he shows us in this guidebook. They're valuable principles, but they are not promises. When we interpret proverbs as promises, we mishandle God's Word and mislead ourselves and others—and that gets us into trouble!

A NOTE ON BIBLE TRANSLATIONS

The 2011 New International Version (NIV) is the version used throughout this study. Because it uses gender neutral language where that fits with the intent of the original text, the author recommends this version for clarity. If you use another version, you'll need to keep in mind that the 1984 NIV and many other standard Bible translations use "man" and "sons" to represent the human race in general.

The Author, Purpose, and Power

Are there timeless principles that govern life? Yes, they come from God the Creator, who alone knows how the world works. Has he revealed these principles to us? Yes, again. We find them tucked away in the Old Testament book of Proverbs—thirty-one chapters that promise to make us wise if we study them diligently and apply them wholeheartedly.

Do you want to make wise choices? Do you want to ward off danger for yourself and your loved ones? Do you want to be discerning, disciplined, and prudent? In short, do you want to be a woman who knows what to do in life's complex situations? If so, immerse yourself in the Lord's proverbs, and he will guide you through the maze of our postmodern world.

DISCOVER THE AUTHOR

1. Who wrote the book of Proverbs? What was his position? Who was his father? (Proverbs 1:1)

OPTIONAL

Memorize Proverbs 3:5–6

Trust in the LORD with all your heart and lean not on your own understanding; in all your ways submit to him, and he will make your paths straight.

 Read 1 Kings 3:5–15.

In Scripture wisdom is a moral as well as an intellectual quality, more than mere intelligence or knowledge, just as it is more than mere cleverness or cunning. To be truly wise, in the Bible sense, one's intelligence and cleverness must be harnessed to a right end. Wisdom is the power to see, and the inclination to choose, the best and highest goal, together with the surest means of attaining it.
—J. I. Packer (*Knowing God*, 80)

2. Soon after Solomon became king, God appeared to Solomon in a dream, asking how he might help Solomon with his new responsibilities. Briefly, what was Solomon's petition (1 Kings 3:9)?

3. How do you think Solomon was feeling about his new role as king? What words does he use to describe himself? What was the attitude of his heart? (3:7)

4. What was the Lord's response (3:10–13)? What do you learn about God from his response?

5. What condition did the Lord place on Solomon in verse 14?

6. *Read 1 Kings 4:29–34.* Describe Solomon's wisdom and its impact upon his life.

Solomon's Failure (*4:28 minutes*). All the wisdom in the world will not help you if you fail to apply it to your life. Learn from Solomon's mistakes!

7. What is the attitude of your heart as you begin this study? Are you willing to become like "a little child" in order to gain wisdom?

In seminary, my professor grouped the attributes of God into two categories: incommunicable and communicable. The first were qualities that we cannot share with God, for example, his self-existence and his freedom from all limits of time and space. In the second category are qualities in which we can share, for example, goodness, creativity, truth, love, and wisdom. This is what the Bible means when it says that we were created in the image of God. These qualities were defaced in the fall, but God is now at work in Christians to repair his ruined image, as we cooperate with the process. —Sue

Wisdom is the God-given ability to see life with rare objectivity and to handle life with rare stability.
—Charles Swindoll
(*Living*, 208)

8. Why do you need wisdom? Are you feeling overwhelmed by some role or responsibility? Are you struggling with particular decisions or circumstances? How might a wise and discerning heart help?

9. Does it matter if you "walk in God's ways"? What is the relationship between obedience and wisdom? In what areas of your life do you need to listen to God in order to gain wisdom?

DIGGING DEEPER

Solomon's brothers tried to steal his crown, and if they had been successful, he and his mother would certainly have been murdered. For the cloak-and-dagger account, read and summarize 1 Kings 1 and 2.

DIGGING DEEPER

Early in his reign, Solomon exhibited his wisdom when he acted as judge between two women. Read the account in 1 Kings 3:16–28. What happened? Why did this story make Solomon famous?

DIGGING DEEPER

Research Solomon's spiritual journey. How did his personal choices affect his relationship to God and his view of the world? What can you learn about his rule as king of Israel and his legacy (1 Kings 1–11; 2 Chronicles 1–9; Ecclesiastes)?

 Read Proverbs 1:1–7.

DISCOVER THE PURPOSE

10. In Proverbs 1:2–3, Solomon explains that he wrote the book of Proverbs so we each might attain wisdom. Then he lists words that describe various aspects of wisdom. What are they? How are they different? Use a dictionary if necessary.

11. In verses 4–7, Solomon introduces us to the characters in Proverbs. Who are they? Are they different? Again, use a dictionary if necessary.

12. Becoming wise will take more than self-disciplined human effort. In Proverbs 1:7, Solomon reveals wisdom's power source.

   • Write out this theme. (Note that "fear" is not terror but a reverent awe and respect for God.)

   • What do you think this verse means?

13. One of the most memorized proverbs is 3:5–6. What does it mean and how does it relate to discovering wisdom's power source?

Praise be to the name of God for ever and ever; wisdom and power are his. He changes times and seasons; he deposes kings and raises up others. He gives wisdom to the wise and knowledge to the discerning. He reveals deep and hidden things; he knows what lies is darkness, and light dwells with him.
—Daniel 2:20–22

DIGGING DEEPER

For additional insight about human versus spiritual wisdom, read Paul's complete message to the Corinthians concerning wisdom (1 Corinthians 1:17–2:16). What else do you learn?

14. The Bible speaks of two kinds of wisdom—human and spiritual. *Read 1 Corinthians 2:6–16.* What does this passage reveal concerning the difference? What is the source of spiritual wisdom? How is it different from human wisdom?

SO WHAT?

15. On what kind of wisdom—human or spiritual—do you rely the most? How is your life affected by your choice?

16. Gleaning from James 3:13–17, describe the life of a woman guided by spiritual wisdom.

• List the primary evidences of a wise life (3:17).

• As you examine the list describing spiritual wisdom, which quality do you struggle with least? Most? How might attaining spiritual wisdom affect your life this year?

Why Seek Wisdom?

hy should we seek wisdom wholeheartedly? Solomon gives us many reasons by listing the benefits of a life devoted to wisdom. These are enticing incentives to take your Proverbs study seriously and make it a priority in your life!

Read Proverbs 1:8–19.

YOU WILL STAY OUT OF TROUBLE

1. How does Proverbs 1:8–19 apply to you? What do you think Solomon is trying to say in these figurative terms (1:8–9)?

His wisdom is profound, his power is vast. Who has resisted him and come out unscathed?

—Job 9:4

2. Do you have friends who lure you away from what you know is good? What do they tempt you to do? How do they entice you? What is Solomon's advice (1:10)? What steps should you take to protect yourself?

DIGGING DEEPER

People throughout biblical history have ignored wisdom principles and paid the price. Do a character study on one or all of the following women. What principles did each defy? What resulted? What are the lessons for us?

· Eve (Genesis 2–3)

· Rebekah (Genesis 27)

· Jezebel (1 Kings 16:29–
   21:24; 2 Kings 9:30–37)

3. Verses 11–19 give us a glimpse into the evil minds of criminals as they tempt the naive to join them.

- Describe their invitation (1:11–12).

- What do they promise (1:13–14)?

- Why is it foolish to trust them? What ultimately happens to them and those who go with them? In what sense are they dumber than birds? (1:15–19)

- How does someone end up in trouble—or worse, in jail or prison? What do you think draws so many people to violence and immorality? How can you protect yourself and loved ones from accepting this sometimes subtle invitation?

 Read Proverbs 1:20–33.

YOU WILL STAY SAFE

Since God knows how the world works, he understands how you can put yourself in danger. You can protect yourself from consequences that put your life and loved ones at risk.

4. In 1:20–33, wisdom is personified as a woman calling out to fools in the streets. If you approached her, what might be her demeanor? Summarize her questions (1:22). What is her heart's desire (1:23)?

One of the most remarkable features of the wisdom literature is the sages' description of wisdom as a woman. In the *Meshalin*, or biblical Proverbs, Woman Wisdom is identified with God, present at Creation and infusing all. She seeks close engagement with the world and delights to be with humanity. Contrary to gender-stereotyped images of women, she is in no way passive but is portrayed as a liberator and an establisher of justice, a lover in pursuit of humanity who, in return, responds to those who love her.
—Lilian Calles Barger
(*Chasing Sophia*, 36)

5. What consequences do fools face? Is there a time when it's too late to turn to wisdom? (1:24–32)

6. What reward awaits those who listen to and heed wisdom (1:33)? In what ways does listening to wisdom guarantee these rewards? In what ways does it not?

7. Why does God allow trials into our lives? What is wisdom's relationship to these trials?

DIGGING DEEPER

Do a character study on one or all of the following women. How did wisdom protect them? Glean principles for your life today.

· Rahab (Joshua 2; 6:22–25)

· Ruth (Ruth 1–4)

· Esther (Esther 1–10)

· The Widow at Zarephath (1 Kings 17:7–24)

❋ Read Proverbs 3:1–4.

YOU WILL LIVE LONGER

8. Can you shorten or lengthen your life (3:1–2)? If so, in what sense? Can you give some examples?

9. In what sense are the number of your days set (see Psalm 139:16)?

YOU WILL BE RESPECTED

DIGGING DEEPER

For a more in-depth study of believers abused for their faith, read 1 Peter 4:1–5. How do you think Christians should act toward fools and scoffers?

10. According to Proverbs 3:3–4, can you generally enjoy a good reputation among your neighbors? If so, how? Is this a guarantee that everyone will like you (see 2 Corinthians 2:15–16)?

People-Pleasing (*4:05 minutes*). The way of wisdom will allow us to win favor with people, but we mustn't confuse that with people-pleasing. Sue teaches you the difference.

 **Read Proverbs 3:13–18.**

YOU WILL BE BLESSED

11. How valuable is wisdom (3:14–15)?

> "Wake up, sleeper, rise from the dead, and Christ will shine on you." Be very careful, then, how you live—not as unwise but as wise, making the most of every opportunity, because the days are evil.
> —Ephesians 5:14–16

12. How valuable is wisdom *to you*? What does your calendar and checkbook reveal? Do you desire anything more than wisdom? If so, what and why?

13. List the blessings promised in 3:16–18.

DIGGING DEEPER

Prosperity theologians insist
that every righteous believer
is promised physical health
and monetary wealth. They
use verses like Proverbs
3:13–18 to substantiate
their claims. Find verses to
refute this false teaching.
Examine the life of Jesus,
Paul, and others for insight.
Write an argument refut-
ing prosperity theology.

14. Do these verses guarantee you will have a large bank account, own
    several Mercedes, and live in a mansion? If you're wise, in what sense
    can you expect to be rich and blessed?

WHAT'S STANDING IN YOUR WAY?

How will your life be different if you seek wisdom with all your heart? Do you want to stay out of trouble? Do you want to live longer? Do you want to be safe and blessed and enjoy a good name among the community?

15. In this lesson, we've seen the rewards and benefits for those who attain wisdom. Are they worth your attention and effort? Examine your life honestly. What specifically hinders you? Rank the obstacles in order of difficulty. What do you need to do to gain wisdom this year?

We have not even begun to live if we lack the wisdom God wants to give us. That wisdom is ours, simply for the asking, and it will bring us a whole new and exciting world! Like birth, it will take time and it may be a painful process. But when it comes, you'll be amazed how clearly things will come into focus. You'll begin to feel like a new creature. No wonder Jesus referred to it as being "born again."
—Charles Swindoll
(*Living*, 202)

16. Identify at least one obstacle that you want to overcome and ask God to enable you to overcome it this year. Pray, journal, or create something that expresses your heart's desire. Remember you must cooperate with the Lord as he works in you to accomplish change.

Envision yourself as a wise woman, loving God and life while having an impact upon others for good. That's what God and the leaders of this study want for you. Together, let's make it happen!

Action Steps to Wisdom

Proverbs chapters 2–4 are packed with action verbs. Each chapter begins with a plea from God. He loves you dearly and has your best interest at heart. He knows that if you become wise, your life will be joyful and productive. But in order to gain wisdom you must cooperate with God by *doing something*. That's the way the world works. "If you do what you've always done, you will get what you've always gotten." So if you want to change, you must act differently. That's the only way to gain wisdom and enjoy all her benefits. This week we'll focus on Solomon's action verbs. Ask God to show you where you need to take action.

 The First Step (*3:44 minutes*). The first step in taking action is to . . . be dependent.

 Read Proverbs 2:1–15.

PRICELESS TREASURES

1. God, your Father, pleads with you in the first four verses of Proverbs 2. List the many action verbs in these verses.

- What do you observe about this list? What do you need to do first to attain wisdom? Then what?

- What are some practical, specific ways to live out these action verbs?

- What is the result if you do (2:5)?

2. Who is the source of our wisdom (2:6)? If he gives us wisdom, why do we need to take action? Explain how this works.

DIGGING DEEPER

Action isn't optional. Read James 1:22–25. What are you like if you focus on head knowledge but fail to apply what you learn? What is the promise?

3. Besides making people wise, how else does God use his wisdom (Proverbs 3:19–20)?

DIGGING DEEPER

Study Wisdom's role at creation (Proverbs 8:22–31). What was Wisdom's attitude as she partnered with God to create the world?

DIGGING DEEPER

Read *In the Beginning: Compelling Evidence for Creation and the Flood* by Walt Brown, or another book on creation science. What is the vapor canopy theory? The hydroplate theory? How do these theories explain the worldwide flood described in Genesis 6–8?

4. By acting on the action verbs you listed earlier, what other rewards can you expect (Proverbs 2:7–8)?

5. What else will wisdom do for you (2:9–15)?

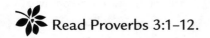 Read Proverbs 3:1–12.

HONOR AND DISCIPLINE

6. God, your Father, begins the third chapter with another plea (3:1). What is the plea? What is challenging about honoring this plea?

DIGGING DEEPER

Read Joshua 4:1–9. What did Israel do to remember how God worked in a special way in their lives? What can you do today to memorialize what God does in your life?

7. What are the verbs in Proverbs 3:5–6? What are ways to act on these verbs?

8. What's the warning given in 3:7? If that's your heart attitude, what's the benefit (3:8)? How do you think one affects the other?

9. What's the action verb in 3:9? What is your Father asking you to do, and why (3:10)?

10. Have you experienced verse 10? If so, describe what happened.

11. Does this passage promise that if you give to God, he is obliged to bless you with money? What principle is Solomon teaching?

12. Sometimes a father must discipline his daughter. What is a wise woman's response (3:11)? How do you think God's discipline appears in the lives of his daughters?

13. Why does God discipline us (3:12)?

14. Share a time when God disciplined you. How did you feel? What did you learn?

 Read Proverbs 3:21–26.

SURE FEET AND SWEET SLEEP

15. What is the action verb in 3:21? What do you think this means?

All mankind is divided into three classes: those that are immovable, those that are movable, and those that move.
—Ben Franklin

16. Again, what are the benefits if you do (3:22–26)?

17. Why do you think Solomon keeps repeating himself in these introductory chapters before the actual proverbs begin in chapter 10? Why do you repeat yourself?

 Read Proverbs 4:1–9.

AT MY FATHER'S KNEE

18. What does your Father ask of you next? List the action verbs in Proverbs 4:1. How skilled are you at applying these instructions? What would those closest to you say?

19. In 4:3–9, Solomon reminisces about his childhood.

- What picture does he paint of parent and child?

- Do you recall a time when your parents attempted to instruct you on an important matter? What was your attitude toward their instruction?

- If you were a compliant child, how did that benefit you growing up? Or, if you were a rebellious child, how did that hurt you growing up?

- When your parents failed to instruct you, what effect did that have on your life?

- Who is available to instruct us all now?

20. Look closely at 4:4–9 and summarize David's teaching to his son Solomon. Again, list the action verbs. What did David encourage his son to pursue above all else?

21. If you are someone who has an influence on children, what are you encouraging them to pursue above all else?

 Read Proverbs 4:10–27.

THE ROAD LESS TRAVELED

22. Where does your loving, heavenly Father promise to guide you (4:11)? What do you think he means?

The same wisdom which ordered the paths which God's saints trod in Bible times orders the Christian's life today. We should not, therefore, be too taken aback when unexpected and upsetting and discouraging things happen to us now. What do they mean? Why, simply that God in his wisdom means to make something of us which we have not attained yet, and is dealing with us accordingly.
—J. I. Packer (*Knowing God*, 86)

23. Describe your life if you stay on this path (4:12–13).

24. In 4:14–19 Solomon contrasts the two paths. How does he describe them? Why do you want to choose the straight path?

25. Which path does our culture tend to favor? List ways that our culture can sidetrack us. How can you protect yourself from the culture's negative influences and at the same time minister in it? If you've found ways to maintain your integrity while still shaping the culture, please share.

26. To be a wise woman, you must guard your life carefully. You are of immeasurable value to God. Solomon lists four parts of your body that you must protect. What are they, and what do you think each part represents (4:23–27)?

27. Your life matters greatly to God. How much do you value your life? Are you careful to protect yourself from influences that will take you away from wisdom's path? If you are careless, try to identify why.

Beware the Snare

In the first nine chapters, Solomon is preparing us for his pithy, practical couplets that begin in chapter 10. Over and over he exposes us to the benefits of wisdom as he pleads with us to get serious about life. But one subject is so hazardous, so alluring, he can't wait. He writes about it in chapters 2, 5, 6, and 7. What is it? A promiscuous lifestyle!

For women, the lure is often not so much the physical act, but the romance—that wonderful sensation of being wooed and adored by someone who can't eat or sleep for thinking of you. Whether you're married or single, the enemy can entrap you and take you down. Why are so many women vulnerable? What unmet needs are involved? And how can we protect ourselves?

Ask God to give you insight into this unspoken snare. Let's bring it out into the light and arm ourselves together.

Solomon assumes that the reader is married, as was customary in his culture for persons from the age of puberty. Although in our culture many marry later or remain single, the lessons still apply. Tailor them to fit your circumstances and remember to change the gender from masculine to feminine.

 Read Proverbs 2:16–22.

A TIMELESS TRAGEDY

1. How can wisdom protect you (2:16)?

OPTIONAL

Memorize 1 Corinthians 6:19–20

Do you not know that your bodies are temples of the Holy Spirit, who is in you, whom you have received from God? You are not your own; you were bought at a price. Therefore honor God with your bodies.

When our marvelous Creator-Lord gave mankind the gift of sex, and when He handled the description of it and the rules for it in His book, He did it all with strength, dignity, firmness, tenderness, beauty, and clarity—all at once.
—Ray and Anne Ortlund (foreword to *Running the Red Lights*, 9)

DIGGING DEEPER

Read 2 Samuel 11 and
12—the story of Solomon's
parents David and Bath-
sheba. How did their choices
affect Solomon's life? Do
you think his parents' actions may have shaped his
convictions on this subject?

DIGGING DEEPER

Read 1 Kings 11:1–3, 9–11.
How was Solomon's life
ultimately influenced by
"strange women"? What's
the lesson for us?

2. What was a common occurrence in Israel 3,000 years ago just as it is today (2:17)? What are the far-reaching effects of this practice? Has this affected you or anyone in your family? Please do not use names and please share discreetly.

3. What is the ultimate consequence for those who choose this path and never repent (2:18–19)?

A word to the divorced: Please do not dwell on the past. Divorce is never God's best, but there are reasons for divorce—abuse, abandonment, and adultery. If you contributed to the divorce, ask God's forgiveness and ask him to show you how to rebuild your life and protect yourself from making similar unfortunate choices in the future. Study this lesson carefully. God loves you and the future is bright as you seek wisdom with all your heart.

❋ Read Proverbs 5:1–23.

4. What is one of "Don Juan's" most powerful ways to tempt women (5:3)? How can women today defend themselves from this tactic?

> If you're neglecting daily time with God, you are at *far* greater risk of falling into sexual sin. That regular time of reflection and self-examination is essential to maintaining God's standard of purity.
> —William Cutrer and Sandra Glahn (*Sexual Intimacy*, 203)

5. Where do these tactics lead (5:4–6)?

> It is God's will that you should be sanctified: that you should avoid sexual immorality; that each of you should learn to control your own body in a way that is holy and honorable, not in passionate lust like the pagans, who do not know God; and that in this matter no one should wrong or take advantage of a brother or sister.
> —1 Thessalonians 4:3–6

6. In the Old Testament Law, the penalty for adultery was stoning. This sentence was often reduced, however, allowing the offended party to take all the guilty party's worldly possessions as well as to make the offender his slave. Keeping this in mind, reread 5:7–10. What consequences await someone caught in adultery in our culture?

> But among you there must not be even a hint of sexual immorality, or of any kind of impurity, or of greed, because these are improper for God's holy people.
> —Ephesians 5:3

7. If you find yourself in tempting circumstances, what does the Bible tell you to do (Proverbs 5:8; 1 Corinthians 6:18; 2 Timothy 2:22)?

....

 Attraction (*4:04 minutes*). What do you do when you find yourself attracted to someone who is off-limits? You'll appreciate Sue's honesty as she guides you in guarding your heart.

....

8. What are some ways women flirt with this temptation?

Adultery is sinful. If there are circumstances under which it ceases to be sinful, I do not know about them. It may "feel so beautiful, so right," as one of my patients once told me, but this makes no difference. It is sin. It is at this point that many of us fail to reflect the Spirit of God. We seem incapable of calling something sin without having feelings of condemnation toward the sinner. Or else if we discover within ourselves compassion and understanding for a sinner, we try to forget that his action has been sinful. We need to become compassionate realists.
—John White (*Eros Defiled*, 9)

• How would you advise a married woman who's attracted to a friend's husband in a couple's friendship?

- How would you advise a single woman attracted to a married man at work?

- How would you advise a woman emailing a stranger on the Internet?

9. What will the offender say at the end of life (Proverbs 5:11–14)? In your opinion, why is this the likely outcome?

10. Does God disapprove of sex? What does he suggest in verses 15–20 that shows he wants his children to enjoy sex in safe contexts?

Sex can be rightly understood as a matter of communal concern. Sex is communal because it is real. Sex has consequences. Sex is dangerous and delightful and tempestuous and elemental, and it matters. What we do with our bodies, what we do sexually, shapes our persons. How we comport ourselves sexually shapes who we are. If we believe that sex forms us, then it goes without saying that it is public business, because how we build the persons we are—persons who are social and communal and political and economic beings—is itself a matter of social concern.
—Lauren Winner (*Real Sex*, 50)

 **Read Proverbs 6:20–35.**

FOOL'S FIRE

11. What does a prostitute make you (6:26)? What do you think Solomon means?

12. What are the warnings in verses 27–29? What are ways we play with fire?

 Read Proverbs 7:1–27.

AN ANCIENT SOAP OPERA

Let's reverse the gender and make the prostitute male—a gigolo.

13. What did Solomon see as he looked out his window? Describe the scene and the characters (7:6–10).

In our nation, emotional and physical affairs are played out countless times every day. For Christians, sexual sin is especially inappropriate because God calls us to see and treat one another as siblings in God's family. For a thorough treatment of this concept, read the book I coauthored with Kelley Mathews and Henry Rogers: *Mixed Ministry: Working Together as Brothers and Sisters in an Oversexed Society.*   —Sue

14. How did the gigolo act (7:11–13a)?

15. What did he say (7:14–20)? What might be some modern-day parallels?

16. Does his prey respond? How does Solomon describe the scene (7:21–23)?

DIGGING DEEPER

Look up words like "adul-
tery," "immorality," and
"sexuality" in a concordance.
What do other passages
of the Bible contribute to
our understanding of the
subject of this lesson?

17. What is Solomon's final warning (7:24–27)?

ARE YOUR FENCES STURDY?

18. We are all vulnerable (see 1 Corinthians 10:12). What is your area of greatest vulnerability where sexual temptation is concerned?

Those who live according to
the flesh have their minds set
on what the flesh desires; but
those who live in accordance
with the Spirit have their
minds set on what the Spirit
desires. The mind governed
by the flesh is death, but
the mind governed by the
Spirit is life and peace.
—Romans 8:5–6

19. Without naming names or including too many details, describe a time when you were tempted. If you were able to flee that temptation, what made that possible? What did you learn from that situation? To help others, would you be willing to share your experience? (Again, no names or details, please.)

In most cases, a person plays with the idea of love, romance, and sex with someone other than their spouse long before he takes any action. Mental adultery always precedes physical adultery. It seems popular today to think that sexual fantasies are harmless and normal. But wait a minute!
—Charles Mylander
(*Running the Red Lights*, 39)

20. We can protect ourselves by "building fences." What are some of the fences you should be building? Do other women necessarily need to build the same fences? Discuss.

If you are struggling with romantic or sexual temptation in an unhealthy friendship or relationship, would you ask God to help you take the steps needed to distance yourself from this situation and enable you to understand why you are drawn to this relationship? If you need confidential help, please inform your leader.

The Power of Friendship and Community

"No man is an island," wrote John Donne. This is God's design. We were created for community, interaction, and companionship. It begins when we're born. Babies who are never touched will die, but those who are cuddled and nurtured will thrive. Marriages without communication shrivel and atrophy. People who physically or emotionally seclude themselves from others forfeit one of life's greatest joys—sharing themselves with others.

Yet many of us are lonely and fearful of connecting. We've been wounded by so-called friends or family, and have vowed to protect ourselves in the future. When we hide, though, we find that we cheat ourselves of one of life's richest blessings. Something inside each of us wants to be known and to know others intimately. God made us that way.

Although most of us would admit that we want friends, sometimes we don't know how to be a good friend. We don't know what to look for in a friend, or how to set parameters to guard the friendship. Solomon's wisdom in Proverbs is a gold mine of truth, teaching us timeless principles on friendship.

If you seek deep, godly friendships and yearn to be a better friend, this lesson can help. Begin by asking God to reveal his personal truth for you and expect God to help you "show yourself friendly" (see Proverbs 18:24 KJV).

OPTIONAL

Memorize Proverbs 27:6
Wounds from a friend can be trusted, but an enemy multiplies kisses.

I have just come from a gathering of women. For three hours this morning the four of us sat in a local restaurant, sharing our needs, our concerns, our unanswered questions—our hearts. Two of us cried after deep confessions; all of us laughed. . . . When it was time to go—as other commitments called—we ran outside into the spring rain, lighthearted as children out for recess.
    —Brenda Hunter *(In the Company of Women,* Introduction)

1. From Ecclesiastes 4:9–12, list the reasons it is great to have good friends and to be part of an authentic community. Why is it important to invest in intimate friendships?

There is a tendency for people to isolate themselves when sad, depressed, or recovering from crisis or failure. I have noticed this especially in Christians! We sometimes have the feeling, "I don't need anyone. Together, God and I can handle it." But God "sets the lonely in families" (Psalm 68:6). This means our own family and God's family, the group of believers in our community. We are there for mutual support and encouragement. When the family or the church neglects to do its part in comforting and encouraging us, we tend to isolate and cut ourselves off from help. Try not to do that, even if you have been hurt or disappointed by people from whom you expected help. Ask God to show you someone with whom to connect.

—Jill Briscoe (*Heart Cry*, 106)

 Authentic Community (*4:55 minutes*). Community and connection are rooted in the Trinity, as God himself is a "we." What does that mean to us in the twenty-first century, with our bent toward individualism?

2. From your list, give specific examples you have experienced.

DIGGING DEEPER

Paul developed many friendships with coworkers. Study Romans 16 and describe Paul's relationships with some of his friends in Rome. What strikes you about this list of greetings? What do you learn about his friends?

QUALITIES OF A GOOD FRIEND

A good friend is _____ **(Proverbs 17:17).**

3. What kind of a friend is described in this passage? What sends some friends packing?

4. Have you ever had a friend like this? How did you feel? What did you learn?

DIGGING DEEPER

Jonathan and David were fast friends in the Old Testament (1 Samuel 18; 20; 23:16–18; 2 Samuel 1:4–11). Their relationship reveals how to relate to one another today. Write their story in modern-day terms. What can you learn that will help you be a better friend?

5. Why do some people want to be friends? What happens when that motivation vanishes (Proverbs 19:4, 6–7)? What does this reveal about their hearts?

A good friend is _____ (Proverbs 27:6; Ephesians 4:15).

6. What do these passages tell us about real friends?

7. In contrast, what can flattery do to our friends (Proverbs 29:5)? Can you think of any examples?

8. Have you ever had a friend who told you a hard truth? How did you receive it?

Oh, the comfort—the inexpressible comfort, of feeling *safe* with a person—having neither to weigh thoughts nor measure words, but pouring them right out, just as they are, chaff and grain together; certain that a faithful hand will take and sift them, keep what is worth keeping, and then with the breath of kindness blow the rest away.
—Dinah Maria Mulock Craik, *A Life for a Life* (1859)

9. What was your friend risking? According to Solomon, why is telling the truth in love still acting like a real friend? What will usually happen (28:23)?

DIGGING DEEPER

What happened when King David failed to be a true friend to his son Adonijah (1 Kings 1)? What are the lessons for us?

10. There are times, however, when rebuking a friend is not wise (Proverbs 17:9a). How do you know when to rebuke a friend or when to
follow the advice of this proverb?

A good friend is _____ (Proverbs 27:9, 17).

11. Can you give an example of a time when a friend's counsel was like
perfume?

12. How can you develop your skills so you can help others in this way?

13. How can friends with different personalities and views help each other (27:17)? Have you ever enjoyed a friendship like this? If so, please describe it.

A good friend is not _____ (Proverbs 25:17).

14. Solomon reveals ways we can sabotage a friendship. Have you ever had a friend who acted like the friend in 25:17? If so, how did you feel? How did it affect the relationship?

15. What is another way to irritate a friend (27:14)? What is the general principle?

16. Although your intentions might be the best, how might you unintentionally discourage a hurting friend (25:20)? What are some effective ways to minister to a friend's wounded heart?

The wisdom of true community often seems miraculous . . . and is more a matter of divine spirit and possible divine intervention. This is one of the reasons why the feeling of joy is such a frequent concomitant of the spirit of community. The members feel they have been temporarily— at least partially—transported out of a mundane world of ordinary preoccupations. For the moment it is as if heaven and earth had somehow met.
—Scott Peck
(*Different Drum*, 76)

17. What else can harm a friendship (26:18–19)?

Throughout the New Testament, there are "one an- other" statements that help us develop close community. Use a concordance to locate these statements and list the lessons they teach (e.g., "encourage one another" is found in Hebrews 3:13).

18. Disagreements occur in the best of friendships. What can a friend do to end the quarrel (26:20)?

THE WRONG FRIENDS

The right friends are a blessing; the wrong friends can be a stumbling block!

19. How can our choices of friends affect our whole lives (Proverbs 13:20)?

Community is a way of life. We don't like to think of being responsible for others. In our natural state we don't like being our brother's keeper. Nor do we want any other person having responsibil- ity for us. Dependency is on the most-feared list today. Self-disclosure is reserved for the professionals whom we pay to listen. Vulner- ability and weakness are dangerous. Commitment is binding and controlling. It is easy to settle for a counter- feit or substitute because of the cost to ourselves in pursuing real community.
—Julie Gorman
(*Community*, 16)

20. What is another danger (18:24)? Why could this be a problem?

21. What do you think Solomon means in 12:26? What are ways to follow his advice?

22. What kinds of bad companions are described in the following verses? How can you protect yourself?

Proverbs 1:10–15

Proverbs 17:19

Proverbs 18:1

Proverbs 22:24–25

ARE YOU IN COMMUNITY?

23. At times, friends are scarce. Who is the friend who is always with you?
How is he the perfect friend (John 15:12–15)?

24. Glance back over the lesson. Are you lonely? If so, can you discern why? Are friends a priority in your life?

A central task of community is to create a place that is safe enough for the walls to be torn down, safe enough for each of us to own and reveal our brokenness. Only then can the power of connecting do its job. Only then can community be used of God to restore our souls.
—Larry Crabb (*Safest Place*, 11)

25. In light of the qualities discussed in the lesson, what kind of friend are you? Specifically, what can you do to be a better friend?

Get Organized!

Everyone wants a life that counts, but many of us don't maximize our potential. We fail to plan, organize, work smart, follow through, and pay the price required to develop our abilities and use our time effectively. Why? Our sin nature would make us sluggards. A sluggard is habitually lazy. A sluggard has excuses and rationalizes why her life is tedious, unfulfilled, and unproductive. We all fight laziness, and we can learn to better organize our lives as good stewards of the time God has given us.

> The wisdom of the prudent is to give thought to their ways,
>   but the folly of fools is deception. (Proverbs 14:8)

> The simple believe anything,
>   but the prudent give thought to their steps. (Proverbs 14:15)

Solomon asks us, "Are you wasting your life for lack of discipline?" He wants to send us to his "School for Sluggards" so we can get more organized and enjoy the benefits of a diligent, blessed life.

PLAN AHEAD

Does God expect us to plan our lives? Yes and no.

1. What is the first step to an organized life (16:3)? Who is really in charge of our lives (16:4, 9)?

OPTIONAL

Memorize Proverbs 16:3
Commit to the LORD whatever you do, and he will establish your plans.

When you're dying of thirst, it's too late to think about digging a well.
— Japanese proverb

DIGGING DEEPER

One of the great theological mysteries is the truth that God is sovereign over everything and yet our choices count. For insight into this mind-boggling reality, read *Evangelism and the Sovereignty of God* by J. I. Packer.

A good plan . . . executed now is better than a perfect plan next week.
—General George S. Patton Jr.

2. Nevertheless, what is our responsibility and what will generally result (21:5)?

3. Discuss the balance between planning for the future and giving God his rightful place as he directs our lives.

4. Do you plan ahead? If so, share your strategy with the group. If not, what hinders you?

5. What is the sluggard's relationship to her bed (26:14)?

6. What danger is there in loving too much sleep (19:15; 20:13)?

"I just didn't have enough time." Yes you did. You had all the time there is. You had the same twenty-four hours, the same 1,440 minutes, that everyone else did. But you didn't have the skills of managing the time that was available to you.
—Alec Mackenzie
(*Time Trap*, 3)

7. What is the motto of the sluggard (6:10)? What does Solomon ask the sluggard (6:9)?

Laziness grows on people; it begins with cobwebs and ends in iron chains.
— Sir Thomas Buxton
(1786–1845)

8. What results from sleeping away the day (6:11)?

DIGGING DEEPER

The Lord describes Israel's slumbering watchmen in Isaiah 56:9–12. What can you learn about the dangers of sleepiness and sloth from this passage?

9. Do you love sleep? How much sleep do you need to be rested and ready to tackle the day? In your opinion, what is a healthy attitude toward sleep? How does too much sleep or lack of sleep affect your work?

PORTRAIT OF A SLUGGARD'S WORK HABITS

10. Describe the picture of the sluggard in Proverbs 26:15. What is she doing? What do we learn about her work ethic? Can you recall a time when this happened to you?

11. What does the sluggard fail to do with her food (12:27)? What is the lesson for us?

12. What does the sluggard say to keep from having to go out to work (22:13; 26:13)?

13. Are you a procrastinator? List the excuses you make when you don't want to work.

14. What will ultimately result from a lazy, disorderly life (24:33–34)? Do you think any of these results are irreversible?

15. Does a sluggard know about appropriate timing? What can you learn from Proverbs 20:4?

To become fully human means learning to turn my gratitude for being alive into some concrete common good.
—Barbara Brown Taylor
(*An Altar*, 117)

DIGGING DEEPER

Look up "work" in a concordance and study the related New Testament passages. What does God teach about the value of work?

16. What goes on in the heart and mind of the sluggard (13:4; 21:25–26)? What is the sluggard expecting from life? Have you ever felt the same way?

The average person puts only 25 percent of his energy and ability into his work. The world takes off its hat to those who put in more than 50 percent of their capacity, and stands on its head for those few and far between souls who devote 100 percent.
—Andrew Carnegie
(1835–1919)

17. What do most sluggards think of themselves (26:16)? Why do you think they are deceiving themselves?

18. How does Solomon describe irresponsible people (10:26; 26:6)? What is he saying through this imagery?

19. How do you feel when you work with or rely on people who are lazy or who fail to follow through? What kind of a witness is a lazy Christian?

One common problem for people who believe that God has one particular job in mind for them is that it is almost never the job they are presently doing. This means that those who are busiest trying to figure out God's purpose for their lives are often the least purposeful about the work they are already doing. They can look right through the people they work with, since those people are not players in the divine plan. They find ways to do their work without investing very much in it, since that work is not part of the divine plan. The mission to read God's mind becomes a strategy for keeping their minds off their present unhappiness, until they become like ghosts going through the motions of the people they once were but no longer wish to be.
—Barbara Brown Taylor
(*An Altar*, 119)

A daily plan, in writing, is the single most effective time management strategy, yet not one person in ten does it. The other nine will always go home muttering to themselves, "Where did the day go?"
—Alec Mackenzie
(*Time Trap*, 45)

20. Who is our role model in Solomon's "School for Sluggards" (6:6)? What does she teach us (6:7–8)? What else do you know about this tiny creature that might help us work smarter?

21. What is the warning in 12:11? Why is this such a hindrance to a productive life?

22. What else can hinder us (21:17)? Do you struggle with this temptation? How does it impact women today?

23. What is the lesson we learn from Proverbs 14:23?

24. *Read Proverbs 14:4.* This is a wonderful little proverb, rich in insight. Can you decipher its meaning? How can you apply it to your life today?

25. What lessons would you add to Solomon's curriculum? Have you learned any secrets to a productive life? If so, share with the group.

REWARDS OF THE DISCIPLINED LIFE

 Organize Shmorganize (*2:48 minutes*). If we want less stress, don't we need to just lighten up and let things go? Quite the opposite! A well-organized life will free up more of your time.

26. What is one blessing of the disciplined life (10:27)? Remember the Proverbs are principles (not promises), showing us the way the world generally works.

27. What is another benefit? Who also enjoys the fruit of your labors? (14:26)

28. Describe the impact and influence of a disciplined believer (Proverbs 12:24; 14:34; 22:29).

Put first things first and we get second things thrown in; put second things first and we lose both first and second things.
—C. S. Lewis, in a letter to Dom Bede Griffiths

IS IT WORTH THE EFFORT?

29. Describe the journey of the organized, disciplined woman (15:19, 24). Are you serious about spending your days working hard for your God and his people? Is it worth the effort? If your life is a highway, where do you think God is leading you?

DIGGING DEEPER

Research Paul's work ethic. You may want to focus on his first missionary journey, which lasted about a year and a half, in which he covered over 700 miles by foot and over 500 miles by sea (Acts 13–14). What can you learn about discipline and diligence? Why do you think he was able to accomplish so much in such a short time?

30. God dearly loves you, and your life counts. What have you learned that will make you a better steward of your days on earth?

Word Power | LESSON 7

OPTIONAL

Memorize Proverbs 13:3
Those who guard their lips preserve their lives, but those who speak rashly will come to ruin.

In the first chapter of John's gospel, he referred to Jesus as "The Word." Through the person and teaching of Jesus we understand the heart and mind of God the Father. Unlike animals, we are endowed with the ability to form thoughts and to communicate them to one another and to God. This is a gift from God that enables us to know him through prayer, both spoken and silent, as we utter the deep, innermost yearnings of our soul to a Father who listens and cares.

We know each other, and are known, by our words. They shape us; they distinguish us. When we open our mouths, we reveal who we are. Some of us are better with words than others. Some of us use words as weapons to manipulate and overpower others. Some of us use words to inspire and change the world for the better. Our ability to use words equips us for particular professions—lawyers, professors, authors, preachers. Mothers soothe and sculpt their children by their words. Lovers use words to express heartfelt commitment and tender emotions. Generals use words that send soldiers into battle, ready to lay down their lives for their countries.

Words are powerful tools. We can choose to intentionally develop our word gift or to neglect it, to use it for good or for evil. At stake are our witness and our legacy. As you work through this lesson, pray that God will give you insight into the way you use words. In addition, ask him to empower you to become a skilled wordsmith, using words that build others in their faith and bring him glory.

In the beginning was the Word, and the Word was with God, and the Word was God. He was with God in the beginning. Through him all things were made; without him nothing was made that has been made. In him was life, and that life was the light of all mankind. The light shines in the darkness, and the darkness has not overcome it. . . . The Word became flesh and made his dwelling among us. We have seen his glory, the glory of the one and only Son, who came from the Father, full of grace and truth.
—John 1:1–5,

85

Many of us have received a particular type of training that views self-assurance in speech and action as the quintessential male position and, therefore, unfeminine. We are more likely than men to couch our words, to hedge our opinions, and to develop a general hesitancy toward action. To do otherwise might make us appear to be pushy or [worse].
—Lilian Calles Barger
(*Chasing Sophia*, 48)

DIGGING DEEPER

Remember that a Christian's words are judged at the *bema* seat of rewards. Write a theology of the *bema* seat of rewards. (Biblical sources: 1 Corinthians 3:1–15; 2 Corinthians 5:1–10; Philippians 3:12–4:1. Books on the subject: *Your Eternal Reward* by Erwin Lutzer, *The BEMA* by Tim Stevenson, and *The Reign of the Servant Kings* by Joseph Dillow.)

Four-letter words that changed the world: love, hope, care, heal, work, feel, duty, home, good, kind, pity, rest, seek, pray, live.
—Author unknown

1. Jesus teaches us the origin of words in Matthew 12:34–35. Where do our words come from? What do they reveal about us?

2. Once uttered, are words simply forgotten (Matthew 12:36)?

3. How much does God value good words? Do most people speak with care and understanding (Proverbs 20:15)?

4. How powerful is the tongue? What do you think is the meaning of Proverbs 18:21?

THE POWER OF WORDS FOR GOOD

5. *Read Proverbs 15:30 and 16:24.*

- Solomon used two images to show us the benefit of good words. What are these benefits and what do they look like in your mind's eye? Why do you think he chose these particular images?

- If you learn the art of choosing pleasant words, what good can you accomplish in people's lives?

 Healthy Communication (*3:14 minutes*). Do you tend to beat around the bush instead of using a direct approach? Do you stuff instead of address a problem? Do you drop hints and expect others to pick them up? Learn what's key to healthy communication.

6. When friends and loved ones are struggling with life, how can you help (12:25)? Can you recall a time when someone helped you through a trial? When you helped someone else? How did you feel?

THE POWER OF DESTRUCTIVE WORDS

Words are the lubrication of the mind because it cannot run any more smoothly within itself than its command of words allows. A man's thinking is exact only to the degree that he has words to make it so. We can think in nothing but words. When our words run out, we come to the end of our thinking; all we can do is repeat ourselves.
—Elmer G. Letterman
(Cory, *Quotable*, 435)

7. According to Proverbs 12:18a, is it true that, "Sticks and stones can break my bones, but words can never hurt me"? Have you experienced a wound from words? Have you hurt others?

8. What happens when a person is barraged by a constant stream of wounding words (18:14)?

9. Proverbs 12:6 describes the power of words in an individual's life. Analyze this couplet. Throughout our lives, we all have received destructive as well as beneficial words from various sources. How do we overcome harmful words and the people who try to hurt us? Who has rescued you?

10. What is so tantalizing about a gossip's words? Are you tempted to gossip? Why do you think this is such a "pleasant" pastime (18:8)?

Stop gossiping about others behind their backs unless it's to praise their walk, their works or their womanhood. Make your goal to be the person whom it can be said of, "I've never heard her talking about anyone else."
—Robin Dance, "Be the one to BE the one"

11. What does Solomon call a slanderer (10:18)? What's the difference between gossip and slander?

12. What happens if we give in to the temptation to gossip or slander others (12:13)? Have you ever been "trapped" by something you said and later regretted?

13. How can we overcome the sins of gossip and slander? How can we discourage others who attempt to draw us into these sins?

WHEN WORDS FALL SHORT

People may doubt what you say, but they will always believe what you do.
—Author unknown
(McKenzie, *14,000 Quips*, 561)

14. When are words not enough? What more is needed? (14:23; 29:19)

15. Some people are "charmers" with their words. What happens to the charmer in 26:23–26? Why do you think the author calls him "a coating of silver dross on earthenware"? Have you been charmed by someone who was not what he or she seemed? If so, share the experience. (No names, please.)

16. Who is able to see through charmers (24:12)? How can you learn to see through them also?

Good words are _____ (Proverbs 12:17a; 16:13).

17. Solomon gives a courtroom illustration in 24:23–26. Whom does he applaud? How do their decisions impact nations? What happens to those who use words for dishonest gain?

Note found under a windshield wiper: I have just smashed your car. The people who saw the accident are watching me. They think I am writing down my name and address. They are wrong.
—Sam Levenson
(*You Don't Have to Be*, 195)

18. What does God hate (12:22)? Name subtle ways our nation tolerates deceit.

19. In what ways are you tempted to dishonesty and deceit? Can you describe a specific time? Discuss.

Good words are _____ (Proverbs 10:19).

20. What do these Proverbs reveal?

Proverbs 10:19

Proverbs 13:3

Proverbs 17:28

Proverbs 18:2

21. Are you a woman of many words? Has it caused trouble? If you have learned to curtail excess talking, share how you became an "undertalker."

Good words are _____ (Proverbs 15:1; 25:15).

22. What kind of a person is pictured in 15:1 and 25:15? If you know someone who responds this way, describe him or her. Why is this person able to influence others and bring positive results?

Good words are _____ **(Proverbs 15:23).**

23. *Read Proverbs 10:32 and 15:23.* Have you ever known anyone who was skilled with words like this? How did they minister to those around them? Can you recall an experience when someone ministered to you in this way? If so, please share.

24. What word pictures does Solomon use to describe these kinds of words in 10:20 and 25:11?

Cold words freeze people, and hot words scorch them, and bitter words make them bitter, and wrathful words make them wrathful. Kind words also produce their image on men's souls; and a beautiful image it is. They sooth, and quiet, and comfort the hearer.
—Blaise Pascal
(Cory, *Quotable*, 453)

25. What rewards await those skilled with words (22:11)?

DIGGING DEEPER

Jesus was the finest word-smith the world has ever known. Study his interaction with those who were trying to trick him in Luke 20. How did he use words to reveal what was in their hearts and to teach truth? Write out the principles you discover.

26. Evaluate your words. It's easy to remember words that build and to forget our words that harm. Would others say you need to talk less or more?

27. Are your words timely and true?

28. At the *bema*, will Jesus praise you for your words, or will you be ashamed?

29. What do you specifically need to do to become a woman of wise words?

Won't You Be My Neighbor?

High fences, long working hours, the Internet, fear—many factors keep people isolated, hidden away in their own little worlds. In our culture, our neighbors can live down the hall or across the street for years and we may never even know their names. In the Bible, our neighbors are not our Christian friends. Our neighbors are the people of the world, especially the people where we live, work, and do business. How should we treat our neighbors? Why is "good neighboring" so important to God? Let's find out.

WHO IS MY NEIGHBOR?

PROBE THE PASSAGE

Jesus lived in a world marked by social castes, prejudice, and religious hypocrisy. One day a religious expert, trying to save face and live for himself, challenged Jesus with this question: "Who is my neighbor?" In response, Jesus told the story of the Good Samaritan.

Commit to reading Luke 10:25–37 at least five days this week. On each day, before and after you read, ask the Holy Spirit to illuminate the passage for you. After you read, meditate on the passage and ask yourself questions:

- What is going on in the story?
- Why did Jesus tell this story?
- What is the main point of the story?
- Was one idea particularly striking, causing me to stop and think?
- Why did God record this in the Bible for me?
- How does this impact my life now and in the future?
- What questions do I have about the passage?

OPTIONAL

Memorize Luke 10:27

"Love the Lord your God with all your heart and with all your soul and with all your strength and with all your mind"; and, "Love your neighbor as yourself."

Hear, O Israel: The LORD our God, the LORD is one. Love the LORD your God with all your heart and with all your soul and with all your strength. These commandments that I give you today are to be on your hearts.
—Deuteronomy 6:4–6

The authentic religious heritage of Judaism and Christianity is primarily a communal and not an individualistic one. It shows how we are to be together in the world, not just how to be good individuals. It reminds us that "who is my neighbor" is our most fundamental kind of question. It is the "way we have learned from Christ."
—B. J. Lee
(*Dangerous*, 120–21)

The wisdom of the Desert Fathers includes the wisdom that the hardest spiritual work in the world is to love the neighbor as the self—to encounter another human being not as someone you can use, change, fix, help, save, enroll, convince or control, but simply as someone who can spring you from the prison of yourself, if you will allow it. All you have to do is recognize another you "out there"—your other self in the world—for whom you may care as instinctively as you care for yourself. To become that person, even for a moment, is to understand what it means to die to yourself. This can be as frightening as it is liberating. It may be the only real spiritual discipline there is.
—Barbara Brown Taylor
(*An Altar*, 93)

Don't be surprised if nothing jumps out at you right away. Don't be discouraged if you don't understand all you read. Be patient and probe the passage with questions. Record your thoughts each day.

Day 1

Day 2

Day 3

Day 4

Day 5

Racial Reconciliation (*3:56 minutes*). God is a fan of diversity. Are you?

NEIGHBORLY WAYS

1. According to these proverbs, how are we to treat our neighbors?

   Proverbs 3:27–30

   Proverbs 14:21

2. Some neighbors irritate us. They let their dogs bark at night, don't take care of their yards, or find other ways to infringe on our space.

   • How does Solomon suggest we treat the irritating neighbor (Proverbs 25:21–22)?

   • What heart attitude does God ask us to display toward this neighbor (24:17)?

The Church has a wonderful message to proclaim—the hope of eternal meaning, the love of persons in deep relationship because God loved us first, the faith that we are accepted on the basis of the merits of Someone perfect and not because we have successfully managed to be the most efficient. Everyone in the world is longing for the Hilarity of that kind of hope, that fulfillment of being loved, that content of faith that will not change.
—Marva Dawn
(*Truly the Community*, xiv)

DIGGING DEEPER

In Romans 13:8–14 and 15:2, Paul instructs us on our attitudes toward our neighbors. How do we "fulfill the law" toward neighbors? What principles can you uncover?

You can safely assume you've created God in your image when it turns out that God hates all the same people you do.
—Anne Lamott
(*Bird by Bird*, 22)

As ambassadors for Christ, we need to have an ethical standard which guides our appeal, regardless of how people respond. I believe there is such a standard. And, simply stated, it is this: Any persuasive effort which restricts another's freedom to choose for or against Jesus Christ is wrong.
—Em Griffin
(Swindoll, *Tale*, 618)

3. What is the warning to us in 25:17? Discuss healthy boundaries in relationships with neighbors.

4. What is the warning in 16:29? How can you genuinely care for your neighbor without putting yourself in danger?

5. Our culture is quick to take disputes to court. What is Solomon's advice in 25:7b–10? Why?

6. What should we do if neighbors—or even Christian friends—ask us to involve ourselves in financial deals, such as guaranteeing loans or investing money in their businesses? *Read Proverbs 17:18 and 6:1–5.* What problems can result?

NEIGHBORLY WORDS

7. According to the following proverbs, what kinds of words honor God and woo our neighbors to the Lord? What kinds of words drive them away?

Proverbs 11:9

Proverbs 11:12

Proverbs 26:18–19

Proverbs 29:5

8. Timing is important in any relationship. What is the advice in 27:14?

ARE YOU A GOOD NEIGHBOR?

Each year at our retreat I'm astounded by how many women say, "I came with my neighbor." Women most often come to faith through caring Christian neighbors in the midst of their communities. We are Christ's ambassadors, his witnesses to a hurting and sometimes hostile world. The term *Christian* means "little Christ," and that's our calling—to reflect Christ in our communities and our world.

9. Why is it challenging to be a good neighbor today? What is most difficult for you?

10. What do you think the Holy Spirit may want to teach you through this lesson?

11. What kind of a neighbor are you? What have you learned about neighborliness to help you reach out to those around you with genuine concern? Is there a specific application you can make right now?

for small group discussion use

Directions for use: During discussion time, the discussion group leader will use this guide to lead her group through an analysis of Luke 10:25–37.

The gospel of Luke: Early Christian writings identify the physician Luke as the author of this book and the book of Acts. Luke was a Gentile, who never met Jesus but heard about him through the apostle Paul. Luke wrote this book sometime between A.D. 60 and A.D. 90. It was written to a Gentile named Theophilus to reassure him that God was still at work in the Christian community after Christ's ascension.

Luke 10 can be divided into three sections. Each section describes a different aspect of the Christian life. The first section, Luke 10:1–24, instructs us to be ambassadors, representing the Lord. The second section, Luke 10:25–37, instructs us to be neighbors, replicating the Lord. The third section, Luke 10:38–42, instructs us to be worshippers, responding to the Lord.

To hear what the Holy Spirit is saying to you through this passage, and to help you observe the facts, you must ask some questions: Who? What? Where? Why? How? No detail is too small. God loves for us to dig for treasures in his Word. This process of observing is very important and shouldn't be rushed. It is through this process that you discover and take away an understanding of what the author is saying. Many questions may come to mind as you read and reread. Ask them, write them down, and look up other Scripture passages to see what you can find. You may also want to read the passage in another version of the Bible.

What Does the Passage Say?

- *Who* are the people speaking in this passage (10:25–29, 36–37)?

- *What* questions did the man ask? List them in order.

- *How* does Jesus respond to the questioning?

- *Who* answered the man's questions?

- *How* would you describe the scene between the speakers?

- *Who* else might be present during this conversation?

- *Why* is the man asking the questions?

- *What* details can you observe about the people speaking?

- *Where* does the action in Jesus' story take place (10:30–35)?

- *Who* are the people in Jesus' story?

- *What* nationality are these people?

- *Who* are the Samaritans?

- *What* details can you observe about the people in the story?

- *What* is happening in the story? (Look for action words.)

- *How* would you describe the scene?

- *What* does the word *mercy* mean?

- *What* command did Jesus give the man in verse 37?

- *How* did this relate to the man's statement?

- *What* else did you observe in this passage?

Now that you have read and thought and questioned and gathered all sorts of facts and clues like an investigative reporter, it's time to move to the next step: interpretation.

What Does It Mean?

- *Why* do you think the man asked Jesus the questions?

- *What* do you think the connection is between the man's two questions (10:25b, 29)?

- *Why* do you think Jesus asked the man the questions in verses 26 and 36?

- *Why* do you think Jesus used the thief, priest, Levite, and Samaritan in his story?

- *What* is the main idea in Jesus' story?

- *What* do you think is the main idea in this passage?

These kinds of questions will help you better understand what the author intended. All of this is key in moving to the next question: "What is the Holy Spirit saying to me personally through this passage?" Here is where you go beyond seeing and understanding to recognizing that God, the Holy Spirit, is speaking to you directly through his Word so you'll know how to apply it to your life.

How Does This Apply to Me?

- *What* is the Holy Spirit saying to me in this passage?

- *What* is one way to apply this passage to my life (for example, to family, friendships, marriage, work, ministry, or social life)?

Blessed Are the Peacemakers

What should you do if a friend pulls you aside and says, "I'm so angry about the way Jane treated me yesterday"? Our tendency is to listen and empathize with our friends. We want to help them work through their anger and hurt. We've been taught that's what a good friend does. But if we're not on guard, we're drawn into sin. It's so easy to take up an offense for this friend and walk away angry with Jane, too. When that happens, the friend feels affirmed in her anger and is more likely to continue talking to others about Jane. This is how conflict is birthed and is spread to wound others and dishonor God. When our disagreements concern the family, the church, or the nation, the results are even more disastrous.

Conflict is like a country road: you never know where it's going to take you. God's Word contains clear instructions on how to resolve conflict, but these mandates are some of the most ignored in the Bible. Why? How does Jesus want us to respond to conflict? What would Solomon and New Testament authors suggest? This lesson tackles these hard questions with the assurance that if we apply what we learn, we will be blessed. Because Jesus promised, "Blessed are the peacemakers" (Matthew 5:9).

> **OPTIONAL**
>
> Memorize Psalm 34:14
>
> Turn from evil and do good; seek peace and pursue it.

JESUS SAYS . . .

PROBE THE PASSAGE

In Matthew 18:15–17, Jesus gave us clear instructions about what to do when we face conflict. Read these verses at least five days this week. Before and after you read each day, ask the Holy Spirit to illuminate the passage for you. After you read, meditate on the passage and ask yourself questions:

- What pattern or process do I see in these verses?
- What is the main idea of the passage?
- Was there an idea that was particularly striking, causing me to stop and think?

My friend Brian says that the heart of all human conflict is the phrase, "I'm not getting what I want." When you're totally honest about the pain, what's at the center? Could it be that you're not getting what you want? You're getting an invitation to grow, I think, as unwelcome as it may be.

—Shauna Niequist
(*Bittersweet*, 234)

- Why did God record this in the Bible for me?
- What impact does this have on my life right now and in the future?
- What questions do I have about this passage?
- How might Proverbs 17:9 and 19:11 relate to this passage?

Don't be discouraged if nothing jumps out at you immediately, or if you don't understand all you read. Be patient and keep probing the passage with questions. Record your thoughts each day.

Day 1

Day 2

Day 3

Day 4

Day 5

1. How does God view people who constantly cause conflict (Proverbs 6:16–19)?

Given the fallen nature of the heart and the complexities of personalities, conflict is unavoidable. How should we deal with our emotions when others are insensitive, manipulative, or just plain mean? Why do men and women tend to deal with conflict differently? To explore these issues, read my book (coauthored with Kelley Mathews) *Leading Women Who Wound*. —Sue

2. According to Proverbs 17:19, how does God label people who enjoy conflict? Why are they so dangerous?

 Conflict Resolution (*5:25 minutes*). Proverbs speaks of four different kinds of people—the wise, the naive, the fool, and the wicked. Sue applies the principles of conflict resolution from Matthew 18:15–17 in dealing with each.

3. What should you do when someone tries to draw you into a conflict?

   Proverbs 17:4

If it is possible, as far as it depends on you, live at peace with everyone.
—Romans 12:18

Proverbs 17:14

4. What will happen if you refuse to involve yourself in other people's conflicts (26:20)?

5. What will happen if you choose to involve yourself in other people's conflicts (26:17)?

6. Solomon paints word pictures of contentious women in Proverbs 19:13b; 21:9, 19; 27:15. What are they like? Do you see yourself in any of these descriptions?

7. If you're caught up in conflict, how will you probably feel (27:3)?

To be successful as a peacemaker, your top priority is to pursue emotional health. Work hard on the inner you. —Sue

8. If you pursue peace, what benefits can you expect (3:17; 12:20; 14:30)?

It is true that some situations are unlikely to improve regardless of how skilled you become. The people involved may be so emotionally troubled, the stakes so high, or the conflict so intense that a book or even professional intervention is unlikely to help. However, for every case that is truly hopeless, there are a thousand that appear hopeless but are not.
—Douglas Stone, Bruce Patton, and Sheila Heen (*Difficult*, 19)

Do not be overcome by evil, but overcome evil with good.
—Romans 12:21

9. According to Paul, what should you do if you find yourself in the midst of conflict (Ephesians 4:15)? What does this mean?

DIGGING DEEPER

Study Romans 14 and extract principles that will help you extinguish a judgmental attitude and pursue peace.

DIGGING DEEPER

What happened in Philippians 4:2–3? What principles can you discover to help with conflict among women in the church?

DIGGING DEEPER

Paul's letter to the Ephesians is filled with counsel on ways to live as peacemakers with people who are different from us. What can you learn from 2:11–3:13?

DIGGING DEEPER

Read 1 Peter 3:8–12 for Peter's instructions on how to be a peacemaker. What is the penalty if you cause conflict?

DIGGING DEEPER

What are the instructions in Hebrews 12:14–15? What can happen if we do not follow God's design concerning conflict?

10. Why did Paul rebuke young widows in 1 Timothy 5:13? Why is it crucial not to act this way?

11. According to James, what can you expect if you are a peacemaker (James 3:18)? What does this mean?

12. Are you faithful in following the Bible's instruction concerning conflict? Be honest. Spend some time prayerfully asking God to reveal your actions and attitudes. If you struggle to obey, attempt to discern why. What do you need to do to become a peacemaker? If you've learned to live by these principles, share with your group the blessings you've enjoyed as a result.

> Arguing creates another problem in difficult conversations: it inhibits change. *Telling* someone to change makes it less rather than more likely that they will. This is because people almost never change without first feeling understood.
> —Douglas Stone, Bruce Patton, and Sheila Heen (*Difficult*, 29)

Table Talk

for small group discussion use

Let's apply what we've learned to real-life situations. Read the case studies and then discuss the questions to help you prepare to be a peacemaker.

Case Study #1

Carol has been going to church for three years. Shortly after she began attending, she joined the worship team. One of the vocalists was a woman named Jan, an outspoken woman who serves in other areas of ministry in the church.

Jan missed practices regularly but would appear on Sundays, expecting to sing for Sunday service. At times the worship leader would make music changes during practice. Jan would learn of those changes during the sound check on Sunday morning. She'd become irritated and oppose the changes, claiming they were changed "without telling her." Then she'd do things her way during the service, at times throwing the rest of the vocalists off-key.

Overall Carol avoided Jan as much as she could. One night during choir Jan overhead Carol talking about a job opening at her office. Jan applied and got it!

The first few months went well. Jan learned quickly and had a good attitude about her job. Then one day, Jan made known the conflict she was having with the pastor of their church. Carol knew Jan had issues with their pastor, but didn't know (and didn't want to know) the details. Unfortunately, Jan voiced them anyway.

As time went on in the workplace, Jan continued to publicize her conflict with their pastor. At times Jan would listen to Carol's phone calls and, if Carol were talking to someone from the church, she would make comments about the conversation. Jan also kept in touch with families who'd recently left the church and complained to them.

Carol felt pulled in two directions. Her pastor had always helped her in her spiritual walk. So the very people Jan was talking about were the ones Carol had turned to when she needed assistance, guidance, or a listening ear. Carol was trying not to be swayed by Jan's comments. Jan told Carol things about these people that Carol didn't want to know and didn't even believe were true. But eventually there was a shadow of a doubt in Carol's mind.

Finally, Carol went to the associate pastor, and he gave her some ways to work through this problem with Jan. Meanwhile, Carol continued to pray that the conflict would be resolved. She asked God to take away her resentment and to guide her in a more faithful walk, as well as to soften Jan's heart.

About a month later, Jan announced she and her family had left the church and started attending another. Jan really liked this new church. Occasionally, she'd feel the urge to bring up past issues, but Carol would change the subject by talking about Jan's new church. Now that Jan's church life is settled, her work environment appears to need "improvement," and Jan has started to voice her displeasure with their workplace.

What should Carol do?

• Why do you think people in the church allowed Jan to behave like she did?

• Why do you think Carol allowed Jan to behave like she did?

• Do you allow the "Jans" in your life to behave like this? If so, why?

• According to the lesson this week, what did Carol do that was biblically correct?

- What did Carol do that was incorrect?

- Where should Carol seek wise counsel?

- Drawing from the lesson, what are some different ways Carol could have dealt with this situation?

- What are the possible outcomes of this situation?

- What are some biblical principles you can personally apply in your life from this case study?

Case Study #2

Wendy's friend Emma has struggled for years to love and honor her mother-in-law. All the while her mother-in-law has continued to be critical and manipulative. Emma has tried to talk to her husband about the situation but he isn't responsive. At one point she went to her mother-in-law to discuss her feelings but it wasn't received well, and nothing changed. She has sincerely prayed for a change of attitude, for love toward her mother-in-law, and for a forgiving heart.

Emma and Wendy have been friends for a long time. On occasion, Emma will share with Wendy what's going on between her mother-in-law and her. Wendy knows that Christians are supposed to seek wise counsel and be vulnerable and honest, but wonders where the line is between friends sharing one another's burdens, and listening to complaining and gossiping.

What should Wendy do?

- How would you apply Matthew 18:15–17 to this situation?

- From the lesson, what other Scripture references apply here?

A person's wisdom yields
patience; it is to one's glory
to overlook an offense.
—Proverbs 19:11

- Wendy refers to Galatians 6:2, "Carry each other's burdens, and in this way you will fulfill the law of Christ," and Proverbs 15:22, "Plans fail for lack of counsel, but with many advisers they succeed." If you were to give counsel to Wendy, how would you balance these verses in light of Matthew 18:15–17?

- What other factors influence your decision on how to handle this case study (e.g., the heart of the person, the character of the person, the intent of the person, the outcome of the conversation)?

- Has this situation ever happened to you? Considering what you have learned, how could you have handled the situation differently, better, or more biblically?

- What is the one principle the Holy Spirit wants you to implement personally?

Case Study #3

Recently Julie went back to her hometown for a wedding. While there, she ran into an old high school friend named Sally. Sally had grown up in a Christian home, had a solid reputation, and had married a man from a prominent family in the community. She had two children and had divorced her husband because she believed he had been sexually abusing their children. Sally shared how her ex-husband's family pulled strings and kept the case from going to court but that she was able to get a settlement in which her husband could no longer have contact with the kids.

A few weeks later, Julie was in her backyard talking to Claire. Claire was recently divorced and had moved in next door with her six-year-old son, Andrew. During their talk, Claire told Julie that a man had moved in with her, and through their conversation Julie learned that it was Sally's ex-husband!

Julie wasn't sure what to do. Should she tell Claire what Sally said? Or would that be gossip since the courts didn't convict him of any crime? If she remained silent, would she be putting Andrew in jeopardy?

She decided to talk to Claire about what she'd heard. But Claire didn't want to hear it!

A few weeks later another neighbor, Olivia, mentioned to Julie that her little boy was happy to have a new friend on the block. He'd met Andrew recently and played at his house often.

As Olivia talked about the boys' friendship, Julie's thoughts were racing. Claire's boyfriend didn't work, so he'd be home with the boys during the day, which meant that Olivia's son would be in the house with this man. What if he harmed this little boy and Julie never said anything? Could she live with herself? Was she overreacting? Julie decided to share with Olivia the "hearsay" she'd heard from Sally.

After Julie shared this information with Olivia, she called Claire and told her about the conversation with Olivia.

Claire was extremely angry and accused Julie of gossiping.

What should Julie do?

- Drawing from the lesson, what did Julie do correctly?

- What did she do incorrectly?

- Some conflicts aren't so clear-cut. What makes this case study difficult to fit into the Matthew 18 formula?

- Drawing from the lesson, Matthew 18, and other Scripture passages, come up with some different ways Julie could have dealt with this situation.

- Where should Julie go for wise counsel?

- What should Julie do now (with Claire, Olivia, Sally, the man, etc.)?

- What are the possible outcomes of this conflict?

What causes fights and quarrels among you? Don't they come from your desires that battle within you?

—James 4:1

- What would Jesus say to Julie?

- From this case study, what can you apply to your own life right now?

Works Cited

Barger, Lilian Calles. *Chasing Sophia: Reclaiming the Lost Wisdom of Jesus.* San Francisco, CA: Josey-Bass, 2007.

Brestin, Dee. *We Are Sisters.* Colorado Springs: Victor Books, 1994.

Briscoe, Jill. *Heart Cry: Searching for Answers in a World Without Meaning.* Colorado Springs: NavPress, 2007.

Brown, Lyn Mikel. *Girlfighting.* New York: New York University Press, 2003.

Cory, Lloyd. *Quotable Quotations.* Wheaton, IL: Victor Books, 1985.

Crabb, Larry. *The Safest Place on Earth.* Nashville: Word, 1999.

Cutrer, William, and Sandra Glahn. *Sexual Intimacy in Marriage.* Grand Rapids: Kregel, 2007.

Dance, Robin. "Be the one to BE the one." (in)courage: Home for the Hearts of Women. Blog. April 7, 2012. http://www.incourage.me /2012/04/be-the-one-to-be-the-one.html.

Dawn, Marva. *Truly the Community.* Grand Rapids: Eerdmans, 1992.

Dobson, James. *What Wives Wish Their Husbands Knew About Women.* Wheaton, IL: Tyndale, 1975.

Gerth, Holley. "When You Get to Turn the Chair Around." (in)courage: Home for the Hearts of Women. Blog. June 4, 2012. http://www .incourage.me/2012/06/when-you-get-to-turn-the-chair-around. html.

Gordon, S. D. *Quiet Talks on Prayer.* Shippensburg, PA: Destiny Image, 2003.

Gorman, Julie. *Community That Is Christian.* Grand Rapids: Baker, 2002.

Hunter, Brenda. *In the Company of Women: Deepening Our Relationships with the Important Women in Our Lives.* Sisters, OR: Multnomah, 2006.

Lamott, Anne. *Bird by Bird: Some Instructions on Writing and Life.* New York: Anchor Books, 1995.

Lee, B. J. *Dangerous Memories.* Kansas City, MO: Sheed and Ward, 1986.

Levenson, Sam. *You Don't Have to Be in Who's Who to Know What's What.* New York: Simon & Schuster, 1979.

Mackenzie, Alec. *The Time Trap.* New York: AMACOM, 1990.

McGinnis, Alan Loy. *Bringing Out the Best in People: How to Enjoy Helping Others Excel.* Minneapolis, MN: Augsburg, 1985.

McKenzie, E. C., comp. *14,000 Quips & Quotes: For Speakers, Writers, Editors, Preachers, and Teachers*. Grand Rapids: Baker, 1990.

Mylander, Charles. *Running the Red Lights: Putting the Brakes on Sexual Temptation*. Ventura, CA: Regal, 1986.

Niequist, Shauna. *Bittersweet: Thoughts on Change, Grace, and Learning the Hard Way*. Grand Rapids: Zondervan, 2010.

Niequist, Shauna. *Cold Tangerines: Celebrating the Extraordinary Nature of Everyday Life*. Grand Rapids: Zondervan, 2007.

Ortberg, Nancy. *Looking for God*. Carol Stream, IL: Tyndale, 2008.

Ortlund, Ray, and Anne Ortlund. Foreword. *Running the Red Lights* by Charles Mylander. Ventura, CA: Regal, 1986.

Packer, J. I. *Knowing God*. Downers Grove, IL: InterVarsity, 1973.

Peck, Scott. *The Different Drum*. New York: Simon & Schuster, 1987.

Petersen, J. Allan. *The Myth of the Greener Grass*. Wheaton, IL: Tyndale, 1983.

Pink, Arthur. *The Attributes of God*. Grand Rapids: Baker, 1975.

Sande, Ken. *The Peacemaker*. Grand Rapids: Baker, 2004.

Stone, Douglas, Bruce Patton, and Sheila Heen. *Difficult Conversations*. New York: Penguin, 1999.

Swindoll, Charles R. *Living on the Ragged Edge*. Waco, TX: Word, 1985.

Swindoll, Charles R. *Tale of the Tardy Oxcart*. Nashville: Word, 1998.

Taylor, Barbara Brown. *An Altar in the World: A Geography of Faith*. New York: HarperOne, 2009.

White, John. *Eros Defiled: The Christian and Sexual Sin*. Downers Grove, IL: InterVarsity, 1978.

Winner, Lauren. *Real Sex: The Naked Truth About Chastity*. Grand Rapids: Brazos Press, 2005.

About the Author

Sue Edwards is associate professor of Christian education (her specialization is women's studies) at Dallas Theological Seminary, where she has the opportunity to equip men and women for future ministry. She brings over thirty years of experience into the classroom as a Bible teacher, curriculum writer, and overseer of several megachurch women's ministries. As minister to women at Irving Bible Church and director of women's ministry at Prestonwood Baptist Church in Dallas, she has worked with women from all walks of life, ages, and stages. Her passion is to see modern and postmodern women connect, learn from one another, and bond around God's Word. Her Bible studies have ushered thousands of women all over the country and overseas into deeper Scripture study and community experiences.

With Kelley Mathews, Sue has coauthored *New Doors in Ministry to Women: A Fresh Model for Transforming Your Church, Campus, or Mission Field*; *Women's Retreats: A Creative Planning Guide*; and *Leading Women Who Wound: Strategies for an Effective Ministry*. Sue and Kelley joined with Henry Rogers to coauthor *Mixed Ministry: Working Together as Brothers and Sisters in an Oversexed Society*.

Sue has a doctor of ministry degree from Gordon-Conwell Theological Seminary in Boston and a master's in Bible from Dallas Theological Seminary. With Dr. Joye Baker, she oversees the Dallas Theological Seminary doctor of ministry degree in Christian education with a women-in-ministry emphasis.

Sue has been married to David for forty years. They have two married daughters, Heather and Rachel, and five grandchildren. David is a CAD applications engineer, a lay prison chaplain, and founder of their church's prison ministry.

June 15th
2:45